**DO NOT REMOVE
CARDS FROM POCKET**

VIETNAM
the people

Bobbie Kalman

The Lands, Peoples, and Cultures Series

Crabtree Publishing Company

The Lands, Peoples, and Cultures Series

Created by Bobbie Kalman

For Andrea and Peter,
who loved visiting Vietnam

Editor-in-Chief
Bobbie Kalman

Writing team
Bobbie Kalman
Lise Gunby
David Schimpky

Text and photo research
David Schimpky

Managing editor
Lynda Hale

Editors
Greg Nickles
Niki Walker
Virginia Mainprize
Janine Schaub

Computer design
Lynda Hale
Greg Nickles

Separations and film
Dot 'n Line Image Inc.

Printer
Worzalla Publishing Company

Special thanks to
Marc Crabtree, who, during a recent assignment in Vietnam, took photographs that gave an accurate portrayal of modern Vietnam; Lance Woodruff; Pierre Vachon and the Canadian International Development Agency; Nadine Evans

Photographs
Jeanette Andrews-Bertheau: pages 11 (top), 20, 25 (bottom left), 26 (top)
Patrick Burrows: page 16
CIDA Photo/Cindy Andrew: cover, pages 9 (bottom), 14, 21 (both), 22, 23 (top), 27 (top), 29 (top), 30
Marc Crabtree: title page, pages 4 (bottom), 5 (all), 6, 7 (both), 8, 9 (top), 11 (bottom), 16 (inset), 18-19, 23 (bottom), 24, 25 (top left & right, bottom right), 26 (bottom left), 27 (bottom)
Naomi Duguid/Asia Access: page 26 (bottom right)
Wolfgang Kaehler: pages 4 (top), 13 (both), 15 (both), 28, 29 (bottom)
Michael McDonell: pages 12, 17
Michelle Raftus: page 10

Illustration
Barb Bedell: back cover

Consultants
Nancy Tingley, Wattis Curator of Southeast Asian Art, Asian Art Museum of San Francisco; Susannah Cameron; Michelle Raftus

A Vietnamese rice farmer is shown on the cover. The title page pictures a Vietnamese family celebrating Tet. The bird on the back cover is a sarus crane, which symbolizes loyalty and long life.

Published by
Crabtree Publishing Company

350 Fifth Avenue
Suite 3308
New York
N.Y. 10118

360 York Road, RR 4,
Niagara-on-the-Lake,
Ontario, Canada
L0S 1J0

73 Lime Walk
Headington
Oxford OX3 7AD
United Kingdom

Cataloging in Publication Data
Kalman, Bobbie, 1947-
    Vietnam: the people

(Lands, peoples, and cultures series)
Includes index.
ISBN 0-86505-224-7 (library bound) ISBN 0-86505-304-9 (pbk.)
This book looks at the way of life of Vietnamese people, including work, pastimes, families, city and country life, language, and education.
1. Vietnam - Social conditions - Juvenile literature. 2. Vietnam - Social life and customs - Juvenile literature. I. Title. II. Series.

HN700.5.A1K35 1996   j959.7   LC 95-37609
                                                          CIP

Contents

A changing nation

The Vietnamese, who number about 75 million, are an ancient people with a history of many hardships and struggles. Today, they are working hard to bring more wealth and opportunity to their growing population.

Many cultures

More than 85 percent of Vietnam's people are **ethnic** Vietnamese. Their ancestors settled in the north long ago. As centuries passed, these ancestors expanded their territory to the south, pushing other peoples into remote hill and mountain regions. Today, the ethnic Vietnamese have the strongest influence on culture and government.

More than fifty other peoples, such as the Muong, Tai, Meo, Khmer, Chinese, and Cham, live throughout Vietnam. Most live in the hills, but descendants of the Chinese dwell in the cities. These minorities have struggled to keep their own languages and traditions.

Foreign control and war

Throughout history, the Vietnamese have battled for independence. They have been ruled by the Chinese, French, and briefly by the Japanese. These rulers took the valuable natural resources of the country and forced the Vietnamese to work for very little pay. In the 1960s and 70s, the Vietnam War was fought between the north, the south, and the United States. Millions of Vietnamese were killed, injured, or left homeless, and at least a million people were forced to flee the country.

Peace, at last!

The Vietnamese have enjoyed a period of peace since the early 1980s. Although there is still poverty today, there is less hunger. There are not enough jobs to go around, but almost everyone can read and write. The government controls many aspects of life, but more people are able to own businesses, work their own farms, and travel.

(top) This priest believes in Cao Dai, a modern faith based in southern Vietnam.
(bottom) The mountainous north is home to hill tribes such as the Hmong, Muong, Tay, and Tai.

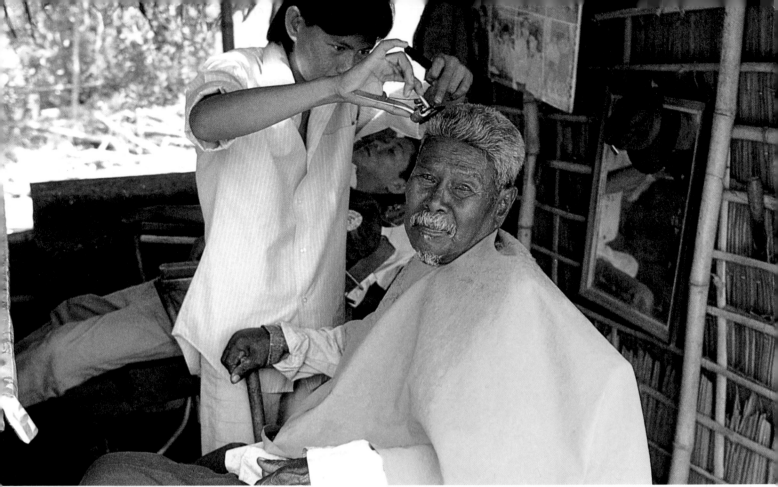

*(top) The Cham peoples are recognized by their dark skin and deep-set eyes. Their ancestors once ruled central Vietnam.
(bottom right) This man is an Amerasian. His mother is Vietnamese and his father is an African American who fought in the Vietnam War.
(bottom left) These women are ethnic Vietnamese.*

Family ties

Family is at the heart of Vietnamese life. Family members give one another comfort and security. Beliefs about the importance of family are rooted in the lessons of an ancient Chinese teacher named Confucius. According to Confucius, the older people get, the wiser they get. He said that children should respect and obey adults. In turn, parents and grandparents have a duty to care for their children and raise them to be good people.

Extended families

The family is not thought of as just parents and children. Grandparents, aunts, uncles, and cousins make up the **extended** family. All these people are very important in day-to-day life. Three generations often live together.

Since both parents usually work, grandparents look after the children. Older children also help babysit their younger brothers and sisters.

Sharing the good and bad

All members of a family share in one another's failures and successes. If a child misbehaves, the whole family is embarrassed. Young people are expected to follow the wishes of their elders when choosing a career or a husband or wife. If a young person does not obey, he or she may be **disowned** by the family. A disowned child is ignored by relatives. If a child does well, family members share the honor. The older generations take great pride in the accomplishments of children.

Family members of all ages enjoy spending time together. This family is on its way to a parade during Tet, the traditional Vietnamese new year celebration.

Sons and daughters

The birth of a son was once valued more than the birth of a daughter. Parents felt that a son would care for them in their old age because boys, even after they married, continued to live with their parents in the extended family tradition. Today, both sons and daughters are expected to look after their parents. They live with or close to their families until they marry. Grown children often share their homes with their parents.

A family forever

Even after relatives die, they remain an important part of the family. Vietnamese homes have a small shrine where photographs of dead relatives are kept. Offerings of food or incense are made on special occasions to honor the spirits of ancestors. Some families also have **spirit houses** outside their homes. A spirit house is built when someone dies in the family's home. The spirit of the dead person is believed to live in this special house.

(top) Family shrines are colorfully decorated to honor the spirit of a dead relative.
(bottom) Young children are treasured by all members of a Vietnamese family.

7

Children

Most Vietnamese children have few toys. They spend their free time relaxing with their family or playing with friends. Children usually start school at the age of six. They are respectful of their teachers and are eager to do well.

Parents hope their children will have more success in life than they had. One Vietnamese saying states this wish well: "A family in which the son is superior to his father is a family blessed with happiness."

Hard workers

Besides spending many hours studying for school, children take on other responsibilities at a very young age. Girls help in the kitchen, wash clothes, and clean the house. Boys work outside, looking after the animals, fetching water, and helping with the farming or fishing. Boys and girls also look after their younger brothers and sisters.

New ways for young people

Some young people, especially in the cities, are influenced by foreign fashions and ideas. They enjoy listening to the latest music from the United States. In some cases, these changes worry the parents. They would prefer that their children follow the old ways and wear traditional clothing and hair styles.

(top) These young people are wearing jeans and look similar to teenagers you might see in your neighborhood.
(bottom) Some young boys, called "buffalo boys," look after the water buffalo.

9

A variety of homes

Families build homes to suit different landscapes and climates. In the north, winters can get quite cool, so small, cosy houses are built of stone. Some city houses are constructed of brick and have tile roofs. In the warmer south, homes are larger and are built of bamboo and wood. They have open windows so that cool breezes blow right through.

Country living

Most houses in the countryside are simple, with dirt floors and no electricity or running water. Villages sometimes have a well that families share, or water is carried up from a nearby stream. Electricity is becoming more common, but most people still use lanterns. People spend much of their time outdoors. The typical village house is likely to have one large room, divided only by curtains. There is very little furniture. There may be two large beds with mattresses woven from palm leaves. Homes are kept very clean, and people always take their shoes off before entering. Kitchens are separate from the main house and are used only for cooking. Pigs are often kept in pens next to the cooking area. Chickens walk wherever they please.

Houses on water

Parts of Vietnam, such as the area around the great Mekong River, are crisscrossed by rivers and canals. In these watery areas, many people live on houseboats. Fish hatcheries are often kept along the shores, but some fish farmers keep their hatchery below their boat. They can feed the catfish through a trap door in the bottom of the boat.

10

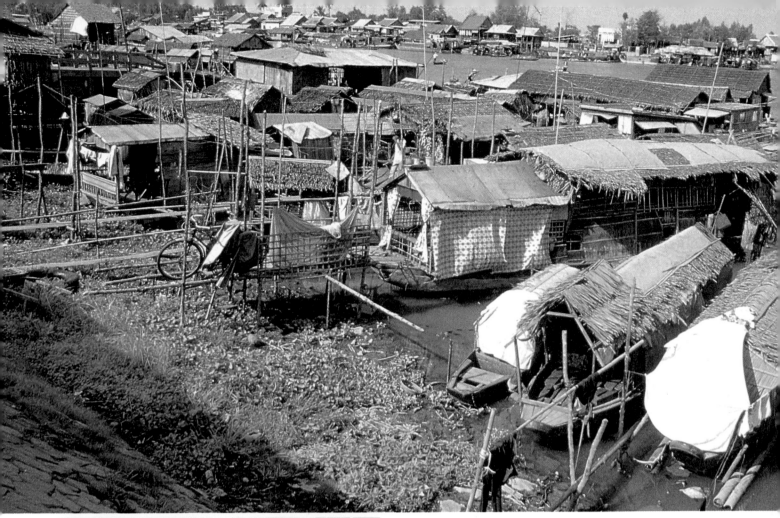

City homes

Most city dwellers live in crowded apartment buildings. Many of these buildings were built more than 50 years ago. In the 1970s and 80s, more apartments were built, but many of these concrete buildings were cheaply constructed and are now in poor condition. Most apartments have two or three rooms, a small kitchen, and a bathroom. Often three generations of a family live together in one apartment! Some families have a balcony or share a courtyard with others for drying laundry.

Like many country houses, city homes have very little furniture. At mealtime, families sit together on the floor around a low table, and share stories about their day.

(top) Many people live on boats on the river.
(left) Crowded apartment buildings are a common sight in large cities such as Hanoi and Ho Chi Minh City.
(opposite page) Country children pump water from an outdoor well. They have no indoor plumbing.

11

Houses on stilts

Heavy rains in the summer often cause flooding, so houses near rivers or in low-lying areas are built on stilts. Although flood waters might surround a home, stilts keep it high and dry. To support a whole house, stilts must be made from sturdy poles. Families use stairs or ladders to climb into their homes.

Stilts have other uses as well. Strong winds can blow under and around the home, so they are less likely to damage it. Raising a house on stilts also helps keep out snakes and wild animals, which prowl along the ground. During dry, hot seasons, work such as weaving can be done in the cool shadows beneath the house. People also shelter their chickens, pigs, and water buffalo from the hot sun.

Mountain homes

Mountain villages are usually made up of several longhouses. Some of the long, narrow houses are large enough for several families—as many as 30 to 40 people. If more room is needed, the house is made longer by building onto one end. Visitors are invited to have tea in a common room in the center of the longhouse. They sit on mats made of palm leaves. Enclosed vegetable gardens are planted near the village. Houses are sometimes surrounded by palm trees to protect them from the effects of storms.

Mountain homes are built with palm branches, sugar-cane leaves, and sometimes planks of wood. The leaves are tied to a wooden frame. To keep animals out, homes are built on stilts or surrounded by a trench.

Not only do stilts protect homes from high waters, they also stop animals from roaming into the house.

(above) The Muong people of northern Vietnam live in longhouses. A hearth, built in the house's center, provides heat and a place for cooking. A hole, built into the roof, lets in light and allows smoke to escape.
(below) If a mountain home becomes too small, another section is added.

City living

Vietnamese cities are overcrowded. Rent in newer buildings is often too expensive for most people. As a result, some people are forced to build small shacks outside the big cities or live on the streets. A common sight in the city is a three-wheeled bicycle taxi called a **cyclo**. Homeless taxi drivers can be seen sleeping on their cyclos.

In recent years, the Vietnamese government has allowed people to start their own businesses. City streets are now crowded with merchants selling their wares or offering a variety of services from pulling teeth to cutting hair. Living in the city can be lots of fun. Read Thu's story and find out why.

(above) Throughout the day, Thu's mother sells many bowls of hot soup. She offers several types of freshly cooked foods including **pho**, *a beef-noodle soup enjoyed for breakfast. Food stalls are popular places to eat.*

Thu's life in the city

It is still dark outside when ten-year-old Thu's mother calls softly to wake her up. It is time for Thu to help her mother and grandmother clean and chop vegetables for the small food stand they operate at the market. Thu's father is already at work. He drives a cyclo.

As the sun begins to shine through the windows, Mother and Grandmother leave for the market. Thu prepares for class on her own. Before long, her friend Kim arrives. Thu and Kim squeeze their way along the crowded streets towards their school. They like school. Their teacher is strict, but she makes learning interesting. Today, to her delight, Thu learns that she scored third in her class on a math test.

In the afternoon, the students go on their annual field trip. This year, it is to the city zoo. The teacher points out endangered animals from Vietnam's wilderness, such as tigers, elephants, and the Javan rhinoceros.

Thu and Kim walk home through the market, stopping to visit Mother's food stall and have a drink of coconut milk. Grandmother is tired, so she joins the two girls on their walk home. She tells them stories of the old days.

In the evening, Mother and Father return home. Everyone is proud to hear that Thu had a high score on her math test. Later, they share the news with Thu's aunt and uncle, who have come to visit. The family drinks a pot of piping hot tea as they chat. Uncle tells many tales about his work as a tourist guide. For his work, he had to learn to speak English well. Soon it is time for Uncle and Aunt to go home on their motorcycle. The family will be awake again at 5 a.m., ready to start another day.

(above) **On their way to the zoo, Thu's teacher decides the class should practice their marching and get some good exercise at the same time.**

(below) **Thu's father drives a cyclo through the city streets, hoping to get some customers. Many people drive cyclos, however, and the competition for riders is great. Perhaps he will soon meet some tired tourists who need a lift.**

15

People of the hills

The remote, hilly parts of north and central Vietnam are home to over 30 different tribes. Some have lived in Vietnam for thousands of years. Each tribe has its own language, religious beliefs, and dress. The Hmong people, for example, grow their hair long and tie it up in a giant knot. The women of the Red Zao tribe wear bright red turbans decorated with pompoms and coins. The men wear black turbans and fancy blue jackets.

Fighting for survival

The hill tribes have experienced terrible hardships during Vietnam's political changes. Many were forced from their traditional homes by other peoples who wanted their land. Some governments tried to kill the hill peoples or change their way of life. During the wars, hill peoples were forced to fight, and their villages were attacked. Today, they strive to maintain their communities and preserve their unique traditions.

Slash and burn

Most of the hill peoples stay in one area, growing rice and other crops to sell. Some are **nomads** who practice **slash-and-burn** agriculture. When they need land for crops, they cut down, or slash, all the trees and bushes in an area. Then they burn them. The ashes from the fire add nutrients to the soil and help the rice crops grow.

After a few years, however, the nutrients in the soil are all used up. The farmers then slash and burn a new area. Today, it is difficult to find new land to clear because many areas have already been farmed or built up. Scientists are helping hill tribes develop less-harmful farming methods.

(above) **In the northern highlands, the Black Tai tribe performs a traditional dance called** Xoe.
(opposite page) **This young girl looks after her sister.**
(opposite page, inset) **Children gather around a charcoal fire to keep warm. Its smoke is poisonous!**

On the river

Stroke, stroke, stroke…Tien's arms hurt as he pushes the oars of his riverboat. He transports rice from farms to a market in the city of Mytho. The trip from the paddy to the city was easy because Tien was traveling with the strong river current. Now, although his boat is lighter, the young man must row against the current. He passes one boat carrying a pyramid of coconuts and another carrying sleeping pigs. The river is an interesting highway!

It has been a long day. Tien is growing hungry, but he will soon arrive at his friend Ngo's house. Ngo lives in a village along the river, where he keeps a fish farm. Soon Tien spots his friend's home. He calls out, and Ngo runs from the house, waving to Tien.

Tien ties his boat at the shore and goes up to the house. Ngo's children are excited to see Tien, who has brought them candy from the city. The family happily invites Tien to join them for a supper of grilled catfish, vegetables, and rice.

After the meal, Ngo shows Tien around his fish farm. He has fenced in part of the river, where he raises catfish and another fish called snakehead. Ngo feeds them special food to make them fat. When they grow plump enough, he sells the fish to a **cooperative**, which in turn sells them to markets in Japan.

As it grows dark, Tien returns to his boat. Under its palm canopy, he makes his bed. Tien enjoyed visiting with Ngo and his family and thinks about them as he settles down to sleep. He has plans to ask Phuong, a girl in his village, to marry him. Perhaps, before long, he will have a family of his own. A partner and children, he thinks, will be a fine reward for his hard work.

Several tributaries and canals crisscross the Mekong River Delta. Often crowded with boats, these waterways are important transportation routes.

Vietnamese is spoken by nearly ninety percent of the population. This ancient language has developed over many centuries and shares its roots with the Chinese, Cambodian, and Thai languages. Other languages spoken in Vietnam are French, Chinese, and English. The hill peoples of Vietnam speak different languages as well.

Syllables and tones

The Vietnamese language is **monosyllabic**. It is made up of words that have only one syllable, such as *ho*, which means cough, or *kem*, which is ice cream. The language is also **tonal**. The meaning of a word depends on the tone of the voice. The dialect spoken in the north uses six tones, and the southern dialect has five. The tones make the Vietnamese language sound a little like singing. A word might have a high, low, middle, rising, heavy, or flat tone.

The letters *ma* are a good example of how tone changes the meaning of a word. If *ma* is said using a high voice, it means mother, but if it is said with a low voice, it means rice plant. If *ma* is said with a rising tone, it means clever, but when said with a flat tone, it means ghost. Obviously, it is easy for someone learning Vietnamese to make a mistake and ask a funny question such as "Where is your ghost?" instead of "Where is your mother?" To complicate matters even more, accents differ from the north to the south of the country.

Writing it down

In the past, only the most educated people could read and write. For centuries, scholars wrote in the Chinese language. Vietnamese was only a spoken language. Then, educated people began to use the Chinese symbols to write down Vietnamese words. Each symbol represents one word. This writing system, called *chu nom*, is still used for ceremonies and traditional greetings.

A new way of writing

In the 1600s, a French missionary invented *quoc ngu*, a new way of writing the Vietnamese language. This writing system is based on letters and their sounds. It uses the same letters that most European languages use—the Latin alphabet. Small signs are added above or beside the letters to mark their tone. The *quoc ngu* system became very popular and is the common writing system used today.

The literacy rate in Vietnam was 10 per cent in 1945, but the government has made reading and writing a priority so that now 90 per cent of the people can read.

(above) *The older* **chu nom** *system was used to decorate these banners. The writing is based on Chinese characters.*
(below) *The advertisement on this sign is written in the* **quoc ngu** *system. It uses the same alphabet as English, but it has many accents.*

You can speak Vietnamese!

How would you like to speak some Vietnamese? It is not that difficult! You can start by learning the words in the dictionary below.

A beginner's dictionary

bạn—friend	nam—south
ca—sing	nón—hat
cám ơn—thank you	sách—book
chào—hello	sinh viên—student
chó—dog	tạm biêt—good bye
con gái—girl	tên—name
con trai—boy	vâng—yes
hoa—flower	người viêt—people
kem—ice cream	voi—elephant
mèo—cat	má—mother

✳ Going to school ✳

The people of Vietnam value education and learning. Nine out of ten Vietnamese can read and write. Unfortunately, parents must pay to educate their children and, while in school, the children cannot help with the family's work. The eager students are happy to learn, however, because they know their future will be brighter.

The first years
Students aged six to eleven go to primary school, where they learn reading, writing, and arithmetic. Rules are strongly enforced at school, and disobedient students are punished harshly by their teachers. Most students, however, show their teacher the same respect that they show their parents. Students do not receive letter or number grades. Instead, parents are sent notes from the school each month, telling them where their child ranks in the class.

Few supplies
With so many children to educate and so little money, schools often cannot afford supplies. Some classrooms have little else than old wooden benches, scratched tables, and fifty determined students. Children go to school six days a week. Many must walk a long distance.

In crowded schools, the students work in shifts so that all the children in the community can get an education. One group of students goes to school early in the morning, perhaps from 7:30 to 11:30. Then a second group comes to school in the afternoon. Often there is a long break for lunch because the weather gets very hot. People usually take a nap after lunch.

Rural schools are bare and lack books and other supplies, but the children are very interested in learning.

Harvest break

Schools located in farming areas schedule long vacations for harvest time. Students spend their holiday helping on the farm! Young people who work on the family farm or become laborers often cannot continue their education beyond primary school.

Higher education

Students who hope to go to university or college must attend secondary school. To get into secondary school, the students must pass difficult exams.

Students who do not go on to secondary school may continue their education at a **vocational school**. A vocational school provides special training for trades such as mechanics, carpentry, or agriculture.

In many Vietnamese schools, students wear a uniform consisting of a white shirt and red scarf.

Earning a living

Vietnam is a less-developed country. Many people are unemployed or **underemployed**. Those who work often do not earn enough money to support themselves and their family. Some must take on second jobs.

Farm work

Most people work in agriculture. Rice is the biggest crop, but the fertile land grows a wide variety of other foods, as well as cash crops such as rubber, tea, and coffee. More than half the farmers in Vietnam are women. Most farming is still done by hand, using tools and simple machines pulled by water buffalo.

Industry

Rice, oil, and gas are Vietnam's most important sources of income. The country is struggling to develop other industries to support its people. There are new efforts to expand industries such as mining, food processing, and electronics. Tourism is also becoming an important industry.

Private businesses grow

Vietnam is a communist country. In communist countries, the government owns industries and businesses. Factory workers, miners, teachers, and scientists are all government employees.

Recently, the government has allowed people to set up their own businesses. Foreign companies are opening offices and factories in Vietnam. Young people want to work for foreign companies because they usually pay well. The government has also given more freedom to farmers. This policy of offering new economic freedom is called *doi moi*, which means "new thinking."

Artisans

Many people are artisans. They earn their living by selling their crafts. Traditional crafts include woodcarving, silk painting, weaving, embroidery, and **lacquerware**. Lacquerware items, made from wood, are beautifully painted and then covered with a hard, shiny coating.

(right) This dentist works in an office in Ho Chi Minh City. Many doctors set up their own offices because they do not earn much money working in the hospitals.
(below) Merchants sell all kinds of goods in the cities.

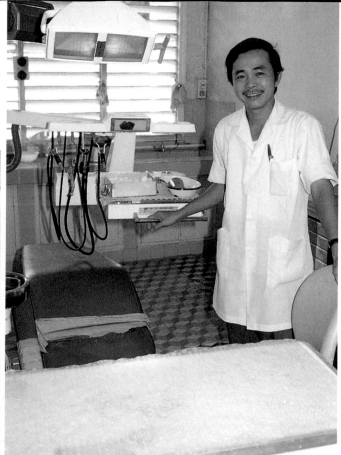

(above) This shoemaker is happy to keep the profits he has made from working at his own business.
(left) Seven out of ten Vietnamese are farmers.

To market

Each city and village has a colorful, noisy place crowded with interesting people and things. It is the local market. In areas where there are rivers, the market floats on the water—in boats! Farmers and merchants bring their goods, hoping to sell them to the local people. Almost anything—fruits, vegetables, clothing, medicine, and electronics—can be found at the market.

Happy confusion

The market opens early in the morning, often at 6 a.m. Farmers unpack their produce, cooks begin preparing food, and salespeople set up their displays. The live pigs, ducks, chickens, dogs, and snakes add to the happy confusion. People stop to buy snacks while they shop. They can even have their shoes shined or get their fortune told. Perhaps they will take home a bright bouquet of tropical flowers or stop to get a bicycle tire fixed.

Bargain shopping

In the past, the market was run by women, but now some men work there, too. Prices are negotiated through friendly bargaining. The buyer suggests a low price, and the seller tries to insist on a higher one. People who sell their products at the market pay to have a stall, but they take home any profit they earn. In the villages, people usually sell what they have grown or made. In cities, people often sell products that have been manufactured or imported. There are no big department stores, so people rely on the markets to buy many of the things they need.

Pastimes

Many people work six days a week, from sunrise to sunset. They have little time or energy for sports and games. They prefer to spend leisure time with family and friends. Most Vietnamese like to visit, and tea is always ready for guests. In villages, people might play bamboo flutes or share a game of cards or chess.

Some village people carefully save their money for a trip to the beach or an historic site. City people who live close to the beach often go there to cool off in the late afternoon. Some are fortunate enough to attend concerts or plays.

Children's games
Children play simple games with their friends. They skip rope, play hide-and-seek, or make up games with homemade toys. They might invent a game of marbles using stones, for example, or kick a can in a game of soccer.

Sports and fitness
For many people, the day begins with some sort of exercise. Soccer is the most popular sport, and those who have the time play badminton, tennis, table tennis, or volleyball. Some young boys are enrolled in martial-arts classes.

City people can be seen jogging or practicing *tai chi* early in the morning. Most people know how to swim, and almost everyone owns a bicycle. People stay fit just by pedaling to work!

Café life

After work in the cities—and in villages that have electricity—people gather with friends at local cafés. They chat with one another, play cards, and shoot pool. Young people enjoy visiting the *café kem*—the ice-cream café. Another place to spend an evening is the café video, where customers see videotaped movies. People like to "hang out." An evening out can be as simple as pulling up a chair to one of the many stalls that sell food and drink.

Television and radio

Television sets and radios are still uncommon in Vietnam. Few country areas have electricity, and people seldom have enough money to buy expensive electronics. Today, however, there are new radio stations, and television is becoming more common in the cities. In many villages, however, people who want to watch a program have to visit a neighbor or a café that has a television set.

(above) Playing board games is a popular way for both young and old to pass a hot afternoon.
(below) The beaches of Quy Nhon are a favorite destination for people who want to enjoy the sun, sea, and sand. Not everyone wants too much sunshine, however!

Looking to the future

Vietnam is at an important point in its history. Many Vietnamese people live the same way their ancestors have for generations. Their lives are based on farming, and their family values are strong.

As businesses grow in Vietnam and more and more visitors come to this country, life will change. There may be more opportunities for people to get high-paying jobs and become prosperous. There also may be stronger cultural influences from Europe and North America. Some Vietnamese people worry that their traditional lifestyles and customs will disappear because of these changes and influences. Other people, however, feel that change is necessary if their country is to become a modern nation. They believe that Vietnamese culture is strong enough to withstand new developments.

Glossary

ancestor A person from whom one is descended

artisan A person skilled in a craft

bamboo A grassy plant with woody stems used to make items such as furniture, musical instruments, and houses

chu nom The older Vietnamese writing system that applies Chinese-based symbols to Vietnamese words

climate The usual weather conditions of a particular place, including temperature, rainfall, and humidity

communist Describing an economic system in which the country's natural resources and industry are controlled by the government

Confucius An ancient Chinese scholar whose ideas have influenced Vietnamese society

cooperative A business that is owned and controlled by its members who share its profits

culture The customs, beliefs, and arts of a group of people

dialect A way of speaking that differs from the standard form of the language in its words, sayings, and pronunciations

disowned Describing a person who is no longer accepted by his or her family

doi moi A term describing Vietnam's new economic ideas and changes

endangered Describing a plant or animal species that could soon become extinct

extended family Refers to relatives outside of one's parents and children, including grandparents, aunts, uncles, and cousins

generation A group of people born within twenty years of one another. Grandparents, parents and children are three generations.

hatchery A place where eggs are hatched

incense A substance that produces a sweet-smelling smoke when burned

income The amount of money earned by a person, business, or country

independence Freedom from outside control

indoor plumbing Pipes and other equipment that carry water into and out of a building

lacquerware Objects made of wood, coated with a shiny resin

literacy rate The percentage of people who are able to read and write

martial arts A sport that uses the techniques of fighting and self-defense, which were once part of hand-to-hand battle

missionary A person who travels to a foreign country to spread a particular religion

negotiate To discuss and decide upon the terms of a deal

nomad A person who wanders from place to place and has no fixed home

paddy A rice field

quoc ngu The newer Vietnamese writing system that uses letters from the Latin alphabet to represent sounds. The letters are combined to form words.

rural Relating to the countryside

shrine A special place that is reserved for the worship of something sacred; a place where sacred things are kept

traditional Describing customs that are handed down from one generation to another

tribe A group of people with common ancestry, language, and culture

tributary A stream or river that flows into a larger stream or river

underemployed Describing a person who has a job but does not earn enough money to support him or herself

vocational school A school that trains students to work in trades such as farming, mechanics, or business

Index

1 2 3 4 5 6 7 8 9 0 Printed in the USA 5 4 3 2 1 0 9 8 7 6